Loose Threads

Sarah Woodason

BookLeaf Publishing

Presentation by *BookLeaf Publishing*

Web: www.bookleafpub.com

E-mail: info@bookleafpub.com

ISBN: 9789357446167

First edition 2023

I dedicate this to anyone, anywhere, who has ever wanted a book dedicated to them but thought it wouldn't happen.

Also, to anyone who has ever wanted to give something a try but not been sure whether they 'should' or not. What have you got to lose? Go for it...

ACKNOWLEDGEMENT

Without Hobbers, this would never have been created. I can't decide whether that's a good thing or not. But it's done now, so I suppose it doesn't matter either way.

Also, thank you to the poets whose first lines I borrowed (stole? I guess I didn't ask first) for poem 19. These are (in order):

Pablo Neruda
Geoffrey Chaucer
Andrew Waterhouse
Imtiaz Dharker
Simon Armitage
Thomas Hardy
Perry Bysshe Shelley
Octavo Paz
T.S. Eliot
Wilfred Owen
Robert Browning
Ted Hughes
Lord Byron
Emily Dickinson
William Wordsworth
Owen Sheers
William Blake
Elizabeth Barratt Browning
Carol Ann Duffy

Edgar Allen Poe
Maria Rilke
John Masefield
Dylan Thomas.

PREFACE

If someone had told me I'd write a book, poetry would have been the last genre I'd have imagined. More likely, a young children's story in the vein of the Black Books episode where Bernard and Manny write one whilst drinking. That bad.

I don't really know the conventions of poetry (even having studied it in English up to Degree level. I'm sure I could have made more of my 'poems' rhyme, but then they'd have all had a similar rhythm- and that would have been so dull.

But since I'm only writing this book for me and no one else is likely to even see it- let alone read it- I don't suppose it matters.

Beginning

I am not - strictly speaking- a poet.
When I try to write things which flow it
Somehow
                    Goes
                                        Awry.
But I have random thoughts which give me a
start
And anyway, everything's
Worth
                    A
                                        Try,
Right?

Loss (Clemency, 2014)

And now, all I can do is dream,
Of who you were,
And what you might have been.

three seconds

Three seconds.
Three seconds to go over the top. To shoot or be shot. Or both. To zig zag blind into the bullets, the wire, the shell holes. Then drop to the ground. With no sound and play dead, or screaming and writhing and bleeding instead. What are the odds? Not great. And if I come back here later, tomorrow I'll just have to do it again. But I have little choice, my fears can't be voiced. Three seconds I've got to get over the top or I'll be shot by a bloke on my own side.

Three seconds.
My men have three seconds to go over the top. To shoot or be shot. Or both. To zig zag blind into the bullets, the wires, the shell holes. Or stay here, in this hell hole and be shot by me. What a 'duty' to have. I don't want to shoot the enemy either. They're just blokes like us, with no choices, like us. Shoot or be shot. The people who make war are safe, far away, tucked up at home. Not facing a mindless no choice of a choice like 'get over that ledge' or be told you're a coward, a 'bloody disgrace to the human race'.

Three seconds.

Unravelling

Sometimes, I fear that I am unravelling,
don't like the directions my thoughts are
travelling.

They won't do as they are bid and it is best if
they remain hid

den.
Out of sight, out of mind, isn't that what they
say?
I feel out of most people's sights and minds these
days.
Feeling isolated, lonely, ignored.

Bored.
So bored with the crap the spews in my brain.
That tells me again and again and again how
useless I am. How useless and pointless - a
complete waste of space. What if I left without
leaving a trace?
Who'd really notice if I wasn't here, if I shuffled
out quietly and just disappeared.
So I keep a blank face. Blank canvas, not
showing the crap in my brain, that takes up SO
MUCH time, almost drives me insane.

Tory Story, Jackanory

Someone once told me I have rocks in my head.
And it's true, there's a lot I don't I don't
understand....

Like why so many people STILL vote
Conservative.
Who really wants a bunch of corrupt,
self-servative
[insert your preferred word] to govern the land?

I cannot adequately express how it makes me
feel
Each time someone says - with seemingly
genuine surprise-
"But I really believed what they said, I didn't
know it was lies"

How can you NOT know? When they
demonstrate how they don't give a crap,
and their policies show their contempt and
disdain again, and again, and again..
It's frustrating- there's not really that much I can
do.
And it's futile explaining to those people who
Can't see what takes place
Right in front of their face.

running thoughts

So many thoughts run through my mind, while I am running on the roads.
The things that need to be processed, resolved, worries that get put to bed.
And the ones that are lighter and just seem to drift like randomness clouds through my head.
Like:
When snails start to cross the road, do they have any idea where they are going, and if so, how?
When spiders spin webs between opposite hedges, do they scuttle across the ground for the first strand, or just launch themselves in the faith that they'll reach? (I knew the answer to that one, even before the thought had finished.)
When bindweed invades everywhere in the summer, what if it took over in some apocalyptic frenzy? Would we need a modern day equivalent of Prince Charming to hack through and rescue the world, like in 'Sleeping Beauty'?
What if the planets didn’t orbit in a well-oiled solar system but swung and crashed into each other on a giant metronome?
If bananas were orange, would they still be called bananas? And if oranges were blue, would their name change too?

Spiders again- how amazing they are. Not only can they weave such delicate beauty - they can co-ordinate eight legs. Would they be so graceful if they could wear teeny tiny roller skates?
If dvds could run in cd players (like cds can in dvd players) wouldn't it be really cool (or just odd) if you could hear what happened throughout the film, even though you couldn't see it?
Why are there so many single lost gloves all over the place?+
When do we stop voicing such questions as children do? I don't think curiosity leaves us. We just kind of forget as we age and 'grow up' which makes us more boring and 'serious'.

Rhyming is over-rated

Rhyming is over-rated. As far as I can see, its
main purpose is to show off an extensive
vocabulary.
Although this theory didn't really work with 'the
cat sat on the mat', did it?
It does also help things scan, and have a 'better'
rhythm and flow,
So,
I guess it has its uses.
But whilst poems can be (although this is not the
case in mine) a skillful selection of words, they
would be happier being free range and organic.

Cleaning (oh I wish I could believe in the cleaning fairy)

I wish there was a cleaning sprite,
That there was really such a thing.
To give a daily dust 'cause oh,
The joy that it would bring.

Friday rolls round, the week gone so fast,
And we all know what this means,
It's time to face the house again-
But it's only me who cleans.

"Let me know if I can help"
is sometimes thrown my way,
But I don't think it's sincerely meant.
And I shouldn't have to say.

Piles of stuff put on the stairs
For folk to take up later
Could be left for several days.
And I am a clutter hater.

It causes stress, the mess that's left,
it feels like it's left to me.
That no one thinks to help unasked
I could take personally.

I know it's not meant in that way,
But really it is lazy
To just dump stuff 'wherever' used.
It kind of drives me crazy.

I don't think it would be so bad
If cleaning was my passion,
'cause then I could do it with great joy,
And grab a daily ration.

There often doesn't seem much point,
It causes me frustration
Knowing once I leave the room,
There'll be more mess accumulation.

Guess I must be the cleaning sprite,
At least in the house I live in.
If only I enjoyed the job,
'Cause then I'd be more willing.

Crack on

Edward Young wrote that procrastination is the
thief of time.
It's certainly a waste.
The things you put off must be done anyway,
But under pressure and often in haste.

Just crack on, my child, crack on,
If it needs doing, just get it done.
Then you'll have more time for the things that
you want,
Things that bring joy and fun.

No more "I was just.." or "I'll do it later":
Do it now, so it's out of the way.
Then no-one will nag you to check that it's done,
Like they do each time you delay.

Just crack on, my child, crack on,
If it needs doing, just get it done.
Procrastination will only ruin your day if
You let things that need doing drag on.

Ode to a tea bag

Somebody's left a tea bag in the sink.
Why can't people just clear up, when they've
made a drink?
There's coffee spilt all over the side,
Granules of sugar, and milk beside (not in)
the fridge.
How hard is it really to put things away?

Maybe they were going to use the teabag again
later on?
It's 'yorkshire' tea, so probably -flavour wise-
strong
enough to take a second dunk.
Last week there were dirty plates as well,
Left long enough for a hard crust and lingering
smell.
I can't express how much it stunk.
Stank, sorry.

Maybe clearing up's a thing they shirk
(Wrongly) thinking it is someone else's work
to do?
I wonder if they do at home?
What happens if they live alone?
Someone's left a tea bag in the sink....

Dedicated to those who leave the mess (please sort it out!) and to those who clear up after them, in staff rooms across the land.

yearning for summer

I am yearning for summer,
Longing to escape the clutch of winter's
embrace.
I am yearning for summer,
Longing for warmth and the sun on my face.

I am yearning for summer,
to move on from the cold that pervades.
I am yearning for summer,
for dry crunch, not crisp frost on grass blades.

I am yearning for summer,
for sweet, flowery scents in the air.
I am yearning for summer,
to be outside in daylight and glare.

I am yearning for summer,
Longing to escape the clutch of winter's
embrace.
I am yearning for summer,
Longing for warmth and the sun on my face.

Fifty different words for snow

Some people say there are fifty Inuit words for snow.
I don't know if this is true, but I know there are a few.
This has got me thinking about how
there are at least a dozen things people might mean when they tell you "I don't know".
"I do know, but I cannot find the words"
"I do know, but I don't know where to start"
"I do know, but I don't want to think/talk about it right now"
"I do know, but that doesn't mean I want anyone else to"
"I do know, but it's got f*** all to do with you"
"I do know but I'm scared of what will happen if I say"
"I do know, but what if telling you means you judge me in some way?"
"I do know some parts, but not all"
"I don't know yet, but I will at some point, and then I'll talk it through"
"I do know what I want, but I don't know if it's the right thing to do"
"I do know, but what I think doesn't matter"

"I don't quite know- there are too many things to consider"
"I don't know if I know but I could guess"
and occasionally, genuinely,
"I don't know"

Kindness

Kindness can never be overrated, shown too often, over-stated.
Offer it freely, whenever you can
Try to treat other people as you would be treated- the 'golden rule' is not treat others how they treat you.
Life is not tit for tat. If you don't like others being unkind to you, by all means let them know that- after all, you're not a door mat.
But then show them an alternative way.
Who knows, they might try it out too.
Don't give in the hope of getting something back- pay it forward. Kindness spreads better that way.
Remember- you will never know what is going on for someone else, or how tough things are.
Your kindness might be the only thing that gets them through that day.
Remember to be kind to yourself also. The things you tell yourself are the things you come to believe.
Don't wait for a thank you, getting that's not the point.
Kindness is one of the greatest- and often easiest- gifts you can give. It generates more and is not a one off, so don't save it for special occasions.

Best Friend

Like a sister from another mister.
And there, such sayings fail-
We don't share a mother either.

I've known you for 23 years now,
First colleagues, then good friends.
Closer than family these days.

Truly a gift, you have blessed my life,
I'm so grateful that we met.
How would it have been, had we not?

Sitting and chatting, sitting in quiet,
Reading, walking or art,
Grabbing a coffee or browsing in shops....

Time with you is very straightforward-
Calm and secure and relaxed.
A sanctuary when life's at odds.

When you move away later this year,
I'll miss you so very much.
But our friendship will ALWAYS last.

Be yourself

Be yourself.
Everyone else is taken anyway.
You are wonderful, as you are, yesterday, today, tomorrow.
Let yourself grow, as you grow up.
Give yourself permission to experiment and see how the things you think you might be feel.
Test them out, explore. It's ok if they change.
Everything, everyone changes anyway (two of the 'three universal truths' right there).
Let yourself feel, be and see every aspect of your 'you-ness'.
Don't avoid the bits you don't like- try them on for size. You may need them for some purpose later in life.
You can't be all things to all others anyway.
There will be parts to you that others don't like- so you may as well be familiar with your whole self and not hide away.
There needs to be shadow, for there to be bright, darkness to appreciate light.
Be yourself, so that you can be self-accepting and self-loving. This doesn't mean think that you're perfect and can't evolve or develop. You'll

be more likely to do both these things if you know who you are.
Warts and all.

(Things that make my) heart soar

The thunder of the sea as it breaks on a pebble shore and rides out again;
Spontaneous laughter, joyful and unconstrained;
The 'plop' as a watervole enters a rhyne.

Whippets and lurchers- I'd home them all, if I could;
The breeze in the trees, especially in a beech wood;
The glow of a rainbow when rain meets sunshine.

Un-looked for smiles, shared with a stranger;
All acts of kindness- these can be a life-changer;
Damsel and dragonflies' sleek iridescence.

Being outside on blustery days;
Morning mists, when all's in a haze;
The flow of a river through rocky terrain.

The scrunch of autumn leaves, sweet sap smell in the air;
Skittering pied wagtails, with their jaunty flair;
Warmth of the sun as winter jolts into spring.

Soft, velvety cat-pads and the flex of their paws;
Birdsong- at any time, but 'specially a dawn
chorus;
Sung evensong at twilight and the peace it can
bring.

These are a few things that make my heart soar.
If I pondered for longer, I know there'd be more.

Hope, faith, love

There is always hope
Seen in earth's recreation-
New life grown from old.

My faith gives me hope
Of God's healing salvation,
Unconditional.

What would Jesus do?
He'd show love and compassion.
So I shall try, too.

Breath-taking

The sight of some things snatch my breath clean
away,
Though I would give it willingly, if choice was
at play.
For these things are not thieves - they are
blessings, exquisite.
Things I wish I could replicate, to share or
re-visit.

Murmurations of starlings as they get up or
settle,
Hares chasing through grass showing off their
fine fettle
A sunrise, a full moon, the stars clear and bright,
The hues of the skies as the day fades to night.

Foxes in fields, an owl overhead.
The arc of a rainbow, shades of purple to red
Dew bejewelled hedgerows, a spectacular view,
Frost covered cobwebs, to name just a few.

Unasked for kindness, some real 'love in action'
Boosting faith in humanity- just by a fraction.
Watching my children learn something new
Or facing a challenge and seeing it through.

Most things in our world hold some kind of
beauty
And we are its stewards, with a definite duty
To make sure it's us with our breaths held at bay,
Not the planet, life-starved from the way we
behave.

'Anthology'

Short on words that I could use-
There are a lot, but I can't choose-
I've stitched together a sort of list
Of other poems' first lines (does this make me a plagiarist?)

It's not quite an anthology- my title is rather misleading
More of a quilt made from recycled words,
a patchwork, a collage for reading.

"And it was at this age...Poetry arrived
Experience, though no authority.
I decided to do it free, without a rope or net
[But on] paper that lets the light [in].

On another occasion, we got sent out,
We stood by a pond that winter's day
The fountains mingle with the river,
A crystal willow, a poplar of water.

Let us go then, you and I:
Our brains ache, in the merciless iced east winds that knive us.

Her father embarked at sunrise.
Suddenly he awoke and was running- raw,
When we two parted
Because I could not stop for death.

One summer evening (led by her) I found
The clouds had given their all
The rain set in early tonight.
I wander through each chartered Street.

I met a traveller from an antique land,
She walks in beauty, like the night
I think of thee- my thoughts do twine and bud.
I'm ten years away from the corner you laugh
on.

Midway upon the journey of our life,
So worn with passing through the bars,
I must go down to the seas again, to the lonely
sea and sky."

Insert

I wonder what you might write, if given a blank page.
Here you are then, use this space,
I'll be an audience for your stage........

Ending

I'm still not - strictly speaking - a poet,
And now I have this odd book to show it.
Often,
My 'verse'
Doesn't rhyme.

Whilst it's been a real challenge to do, it
Got me thinking in ways that are new- it
Was definitely
Worth
Trying.

Although I can't see it being repeated.....

www.ingramcontent.com/pod-product-compliance
Lightning Source LLC
Chambersburg PA
CBHW051750130826
49812CB00033B/1087
9789357446167